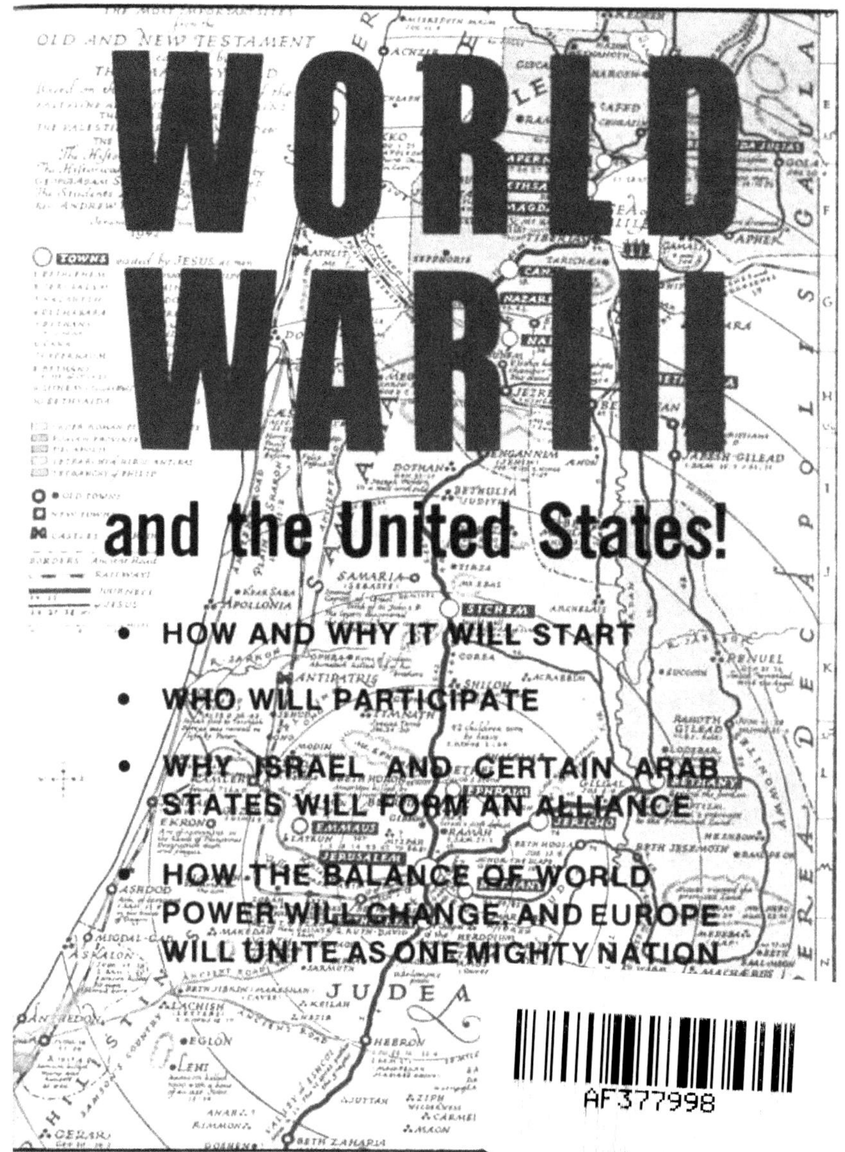

STARTLING NEW DISCOVERIES !

WORLD WAR III
and the United States!

HOW AND WHY IT WILL START

WHO WILL PARTICIPATE

WHY ISRAEL AND CERTAIN ARAB STATES WILL FORM AN ALLIANCE

HOW THE BALANCE OF WORLD POWER WILL CHANGE AND EUROPE WILL UNITE AS ONE MIGHTY NATION

W.S. McBIRNIE, Ph.D.

ISBN: 978-2-925611-53-0
Printed in the USA.

www.ultimatumeditions.com

Dr. McBirnie standing before the Israeli monument to the fulfillment of Ezekiel's prophecy in Chapters 36 and 37 concerning Israel's regathering.

WORLD WAR III
AND THE UNITED STATES

Introduction

One does not need to consult the Bible's ancient prophecies to know that a confrontation between the Western world and the Soviet bloc is inevitable in the Middle East. The oil and food resources, the strategic location of the Suez, the Holy Lands and the minerals of the Dead Sea, are but a few of the desirable things which could attempt a voracious, imperialist power, such as the Soviet Union, to engage in a war of conquest if she were driven by an internal need, or if she were to be tempted by an apparent weakness of will to resist by the Western powers. Who among Middle Eastern powers could stop Russia?

Nevertheless it is highly significant that the prophet Ezekiel claimed that he received from God himself a prediction that such a Russian-incited invasion would indeed take place at a distant future time when Israel had again become a nation and her people gathered from many nations.

We could suppose that this prophecy has already been fulfiilled, but history shows it has not. We could also suppose that Ezekiel was mistaken. But too many prophecies of the Bible have indeed been literally fulfilled for a believing Jew or Christian to accept that idea. A great monument stands in Israel commemorating the actual fuifillment of Ezekiel's prophecies as recorded in Ezekiel 36 and 37. This monument carries the quotation from that section of Ezekiel's writings to the effect that God would gather Israel from the nation and restore the people to this ancient land. This has been fulfilled in our own times!

But let the reader look at the next two chapters of Ezekiel's prophecy. What is to happen in the days of Israel's return?

An amazing story unfolds. It tells of nations led by the Soviet Union who will invade Israel. That story carefully documented is told in the book. It should interest every American. Not only has the United States-guaranteed Israel's security, but the only place in the Bible where the United States is clearly referred to, by ancient designations in Ezekiel's own terms, is in the 38th chapter of Ezekiel.

If this *seems* impossible, then the reader is invited to search the Scriptures as illuminated by the findings of archeologists, to see if these things be so.

If they are as we have suggested, does this not have a specific bearing upon America's foreign policy and military preparedness? If America is really going to be present in a Middle Eastern war, then does not this indicate that we should take this prophecy seriously and consult its implications for the future?

W. S. McBirnie
California Graduate
School of Theology
Glendale, California

The Coming Titanic Struggle
for the Middle East

Surely it must be evident that the closer we get to the fulfillment of a Biblical prophecy, the more light will break forth upon it. As an example: In Ezekiel 38, Ethiopia and Libya are declared to someday become the allies of the Soviet-led confederacy which is to invade the Holy Land in the days of Israel's return from the *diaspora*. Only ten years ago the governments of both countries seemed firmly established in the Western camp. Today, both are completely dominated by the Soviet Union.

Still another example: In the first edition of the Scofield Bible, the footnote on Ezekiel 38 correctly identifies the Soviet Union as the future invader of Israel. But nowhere in the Scofield notes are the reasons or motivation of Russia mentioned. Yet that motivation is stated by Ezekiel in Chapter 38 as, "I will . . . put hooks into thy jaws and I will bring thee forth (Ezek. 38:4) . . . thou shalt come from thy place out of the north parts (Ezek. 38:15) . . . like a cloud to cover the land (38:16) . . . to carry away silver and gold, to take away cattle and goods, to take a great spoil." The value of Middle Eastern petroleum was of course unknown in Ezekiel's day, and remained so until recently. Petroleum is the greatest prize in today's world.

We face the grave fact that modern civilization is wholly dependent upon energy. The greatest concentrations of petroleum energy in the world are in the Middle Eastern oil states. Standing between several of them and the Soviets, with their lust for conquest and potential recurrent famine conditions, are Jordan and Israel, the Arab oil states, the United States, and to some measure, Western Europe.

Every day's news brings this great confrontation even more into likelihood. Events are fulfilling prophetic conditions with rapidity. Confrontation between the Soviet-led nations and the Western powers in the Middle East looms as a certainty.

Is the Battle Described in Ezekiel 38-39 "The Battle of Armageddon?"

Regrettably, this interpretation, which is without much reason for being, has so colored the widely-published evangelical commentaries that the possibility of the fulfillment of this prophecy *long before Armageddon* has not had the wide attention among conservative scholars which it deserves. World affairs which are even now setting the stage for the battle described in Ezekiel 38 are too often ignored as having no immediate meaning in relation to Biblical prophecy. This is an error which must be rectified.

Why *cannot* the battle in the 38th chapter of Ezekiel refer to Armageddon? There are at least nine major differences between them.

(1) The different locations of the battles; (2) the different opponents; (3) the different outcomes; (4) the different aftermaths; (5) the different purposes; (6) the different consequences; i.e., the shift in the balance of world power which will occur with five-sixths of the Soviet confederacy invading Army destroyed; (7) the invasion and the defeat of the Soviet Armies will furnish the climate for the *rise* of the Antichrist; (8) the climax of Armageddon, on the other hand, spells the *doom* of the Antichrist; (9) the building of the temple, which logically follows chapters 38-39 as described in Ezekiel 40-48, is nowhere declared to be the result of Christ's second coming, but very naturally could follow the defeat of the Soviet-led confederacy as depicted in Ezekiel 38-39.

After the invasion of Israel, according to the prophecy in the Book of Daniel, there is to be a time lapse of about three and a half years, after which the Jews are to make a seven-year covenant with the Antichrist to allow them to rebuild their temple. Having then done so, their covenant is to be "broken in the midst thereof," and the Antichrist is to declare *himself* to be the Messiah at the time of the opening of the temple. This is explained in Daniel 7:25 and confirmed in II Thess. 2:3,4,5, where St. Paul refers to the Antichrist as appearing in the "temple of God."

All this would be difficult to harmonize if the battle of Ezekiel were in fact to be the same as Armageddon. But it simply is not possible, regardless of what other scholars have written.

World Super Powers Today

There are, at present, only two super powers, the USA and the USSR. Africa is no power at all; India lacks military might; China is a potential, but not an actual super power. Europe is disunited and its constituent nations are frequently at odds with each other.

When the USSR makes its desperate gamble for the energy of the Middle East, it will perhaps be impelled, as we have suggested, by lust for strategic conquest plus the desire to control one of the major energy sources of the world as a bargaining pawn for food. Exportable food supplies are now controlled 85% by the USA and Canada.

When Russia is ultimately defeated, there will be a serious shift in the balance of world power. Then there will exist an emerging China and the USA.

Europe, now playing with the idea of a Common Market, will certainly then realize that, if it unites, it can become the *third* great world power! By such a union it will possess the technology and resources to guard against conquest by Red China or any organized combination of lesser nations and even against economic competition by the USA.

A person would have to be imperceptive and dull of wit indeed to fail to see that this state of affairs is made to order for the brilliant statesman, the opportunity who will emerge from out of one of the nations of the former Greek and Roman empires. The Bible indicates this person will be the Antichrist. Because of his success in reestablishing a united Europe like that of ancient Rome, inspired by Satan, he has hopes of bringing peace by a new balance of world power based upon a united Europe, standing well above a defeated Russia, an emerging China and a triumphant USA.

The revival of the Greek and Roman Empires and a *new* Europe is a dead certainty by the measurements both of the prophecies of Daniel and the stern reality of the yearnings of a United Europe determined never again to be a pawn between East and West, between the oil countries and the prosperous Americas.

Europe, as Hitler showed, *can,* if it is forced, be self-sufficient, powerful in economics, food and in military might. Though it is sick and disunited today, Europe with its huge total population can become the mightiest single power on earth in every sense of the word. Under the Antichrist, with the Soviet Union no longer complicating things, it will do just that.

Thus, what I have sketched here is a possible scenario for things to come, logical and likely. It also fits the shape of things to come as predicted in the prophetic Word, especially as reflected in Ezekiel 38-39, which forms one of the most specific and datable prophecies in the Bible.

The Specific Parameters
of Ezekiel's Prophecy

For our purposes, in order to see the full meaning of the great invasion described in Ezekiel 38, we need the answers to four questions:

1. Who are the nations mentioned?
2. What are they to do?
3. What is the outcome?
4. What is the period of time actually indicated?

The last three questions are easily determined. There is to be an invasion of Israel by a confederacy of northern European (Soviet) led nations in the era after Israel is gathered out of the various countries of the world and restored to its historic land.

This Soviet-led confederacy is to lose five-sixths of its forces and also suffer great destruction in its homeland. All of this, as we have shown, will result in a radical shift in the balance of world power. Europe will be shaken by the threats of its main energy sources and the possibility of the triumph of Communism. As a consequence it will unite, saying, "Never again!" This will be caused by the Antichrist, the ruler who seeks world power and who promises security and prosperity if only all power is given to him. A Europe thus united will be an ideal base for his lust for world empire.

The Identification of the Nations Who Will Engage in World War III in Israel and Jordan

Having just returned from the Middle East on a fact-finding mission, I was careful to look at the world situation as it is reflected in the growing crisis in the Middle East. In order to understand it from the long-range point of view, turn in your Bible to the 38th chapter of the Book of Ezekiel. I have researched very carefully in the lexicons, commentaries, the Bible dictionaries and the Bible encyclopedias, in order to check out every important word which appears in the 38th and 39th chapters of Ezekiel. I have preached on these two chapters possibly 10 times in the last ten years, but events in the Middle East are moving so rapidly that it is obvious that we are seeing amazing changes which bring the fulfillment of this tremendous prophetic passage of God's word ever nearer, with startling implications for us all.

The message of this book is to some readers perhaps new and strange. We must remember that the Book of Ezekiel was written (c. 575 B.C.) in Babylon by Ezekiel, who was both a priest and a prophet. He was also a great writer of Scripture. Ezekiel had been in Babylon for a long time as a captive. God moved across his mind as a harpist moves his fingers across the strings of a harp, to reveal the truth of what was someday going to happen to the nations with whom Israel is related. We must not think that Ezekiel wrote only for his own day for that is easily disproven.

Ezekiel mentions great nations which, in his day, were not yet born in their modern form. But more importantly for this study we should realize that Ezekiel refers to these areas, countries and peoples by *names which were familiar to him*. The task, therefore, which we have in correctly understanding this portion of the Book of Ezekiel is to know what he *meant* by the names which he uses. It will do little good for us to recognize them only by their current or modern names because the names by which we know them may be modern in origin, and the contemporaneous geographical and political boundaries may have changed many times during the centuries since Ezekiel wrote. The question is, "What did those names of the nations mean to Ezekiel *in his day and time?*"

Then, projecting to the date of the far distant future era which is very carefully identified by Ezekiel, we ask which of those nations today occupies the particular places he had in mind? What does Ezekiel tell us is going to take place among them? We read from Ezekiel 38:1 the ancient tribal names,

> *"The Word of the Lord came unto me saying, Son of Man set thy face,"* (This is a typical Biblical description of the

prophet who is being commanded to denounce a nation or a people. In other words, Ezekiel was told to deliver a prophecy against a nation or a group of nations.)

"Against Gog" (the name the Lord gave the leading person, the dictator, the 'prince,' as he addresses him through the prophecy.) *"Of the land of Magog"* (Here we are on firm ground for Magog was the grandson of Noah and his descendants settled in what is now called Russia.) St. Ambrose in *De Excessu Fratris*, A.D. 378, identified Magog as the Goths. In the Talmud (L Gensburg, 1889/58) Magog is the country of the White Huns or southern Russia. Josephus correctly identified Magog with the Scythians. (S.J. 1,6,25)

"The chief prince of Meshech and Tubal." (So it reads in the King James Version, but in the revised version, correctly, it reads, *"Set thy face against Gog of the land of Magog, of Rosh, Meshech and Tubal."*) The name 'Rosh' is a proper name and has been mistranslated in the K.J.V. as 'chief prince.' It does not take too much imagination to realize that this particular string of names in Ezekiel 38-39 has to do with nations and peoples who in the day of Ezekiel were settled in what we now call the Soviet Union. This is no fantasy. You will notice that in the footnotes in the Scofield Bible which comment on Ezekiel 38 you will find this very same interpretation. There it says, 'the reference is to the powers in the north of Europe headed by Russia.' So, therefore, with that alone we would have enough to indicate that prominent Bible scholars believe that Russia is meant. But we will not stop there nor be content with that, because we also have here the root of the name Russia — 'Rosh.' We realize that vowels in names may change but often their consonants remain the same. Meshech is, of course, related to Muscovy, and that was the name of the tribe that eventually chose 'Moscow' as its capital. 'Tubal,' also mentioned here, was the name of the tribe that eventually chose 'Tobolsk' as its capital city.

"ROSH. This name does not appear in the King James Version for the reason that the King James translators did not realize that 'Rosh' (in Ezekiel 38:3) was a *name*. Instead they translated 'Rosh' as 'Chief Prince.' Of the fact that 'Rosh' is a proper name, William Kelly, in *Notes on Ezekiel* (pp. 192-193) says: 'It is true that 'Rosh,' when the context requires it to be a common appellative, means 'head,' or 'chief.' But it is this sense which in the present instance brings in confusion. There can be no doubt therefore that it must be taken as a proper name, and here not as a man as in Genesis 26:2, if the common reading stands, but as a *race*. This at once furnishes a suitable sense, which is strengthened by the term which precedes it as well as by those that follow . . . Meshech and Tubal fix Rosh as meaning a Gentile name *Rosh*."

As to the identification of 'Rosh,' it is not hard to see that we are here very near the language root of Russia. But that alone is not enough.

Dr. Louis Bauman, wrote:

"Our Lord's own Bible, the Septuagint, speaks of 'Gog' as 'the prince of Rosh.' If modern lexicographers are consulted as to what nation now represents 'Rosh,' nearly all of them, together with most expositors, say, *Russia.*"—*Russian Events in the Light of Bible Prophecy*, p. 24

Robert Lowth, Bishop of London, observed:

"Rosh, taken as a proper name in Ezekiel, signifies the inhabitants of Scythia, from whom the modern Russians derived their modern name." — *Bauman*, op. cit., p. 24

Again Bauman writes:

"The German Protestant Hebraist, Gesenius, whose Hebrew Lexicon has never been superseded, says that 'Gog' is undoubtedly the *Russians*. He declared that Rosh was a designation for the tribes then north of the Taurus mountains, dwelling in the neighborhood of the Volga. He also said that in that name and tribe we have the first trace in history of the 'Rus,' or Russian nation." — Op. cit., p. 24

The identification of "Rosh" is confirmed by the associated names which follow:

MAGOG. The land of Gog, the leader (literally, "Mountain") is called Magog. Here again we are on firm ground in identifying the Soviet Union in this prophecy.

Dr. Gaebelein says:

"Magog's land was located in what is called today the Caucasus and the adjoining steppes . . . the ancient Scythians." — *The Prophet Ezekiel*, p. 257

Dr. Bauman adds:

"Josephus said, 'Magog founded those that from him were named Magogites but who by the Greeks were called Scythians. The Scythians themselves have a tradition that their ancestors originally came forth from Araxes, in Armenia." (i.e., that part of Armenia which is in the Soviet Union now)

The Japhetic race (Japheth was the father of Magog, Gen. 10:1,2), comprised those whom the Greeks called, "Sarmatians" — a mixture of Medes and Scythians who emigrated in small bands to the region of the Black Sea and extended from the Baltic to the Urals . . . today their descendants are known as Tartars, Cossacks, Finns, Kalmuks and Mongols.

The New Schaff-Herzog Encyclopedia of Religious Knowledge says:

"A stricter geographical location would place Magog's dwelling between Armenia and Media, perhaps on the shores of the Araxes. But the people seem to have extended farther north across the Caucasus, filling there the extreme northern horizon of the Hebrews. (Ezekiel 38:15, 39:2) This is the way Meshech and Tubal are often mentioned in the Assyrian inscriptions (Mushku and Tabal, Gk. Moschoi and Tibarenoi)" (Vo. V, Pg. 14). — *"Things to come,"* p. 328

MESHECH. According to Bauman, Gesenius, the Hebrew lexicographer, also, identified *Meshech* as *"Moscow"* or Muscovy. Russians are known as "Muscovites," a name which comes from the root, *Meshech*.

TUBAL. Gesenius also identified Tubal as a part of Russia, (Tobolsk) the earliest province of Asiatic Russia to be colonized. Moscow was a district as well as a city. So, apparently was Tobolsk. Moscow or Moscovy is of Europe; Tobolsk is of Asia. The Soviet Union encompasses them both. Hence MAGOG is the designated name in the Bible of the united Asiatic *and* European Soviet Union, consisting of Rosh, Meshech and Tubal. Speaking of the migration of some Asiatics who were originally of *Tubal,* Rev. W. M. H. Milner, in "The Russian Chapters of Ezekiel," says:

"The historian Gibbon, in the forty-second chapter of his *Decline and Fall of the Roman Empire,* referring to the middle of the sixth century A.D., deals with the question thus:

"The wild people who dwelt or wandered in the plains of Russia, Lithuania and Poland might be reduced, in the age of Justinian, under the two great families of the Bulgarians and the Sclavonians. According to the Greek writers the former, who touched the Euxine and the lake Maeotic, derived from the Huns their name or descent; and it is needless to renew the simple and well-known picture of Tartar manners. They were bold and dextrous archers, who drank the milk and feasted on the flesh of their horses."

Then says God to Ezekiel, *"Prophesy against him."* (that is to the prince who heads this confederation of people) "And say, *Thus saith the Lord God, Behold, I am against thee, O Gog, the prince of Rosh, Meshech and Tubal: And I will turn thee back and put hooks into thy jaws:* (that is another familiar Biblical phrase frequently used. It simply means the same thing that a rider of a horse does when he puts bits into the mouth of the horse, or a fisherman when he puts a hook into the mouth of the fish. It means control by force. This force is to be the motivation which draws the Confederacy south.)

The prophecy continues by naming more allied nations listed with those that have already been named as the chief movers in this great invasion army. In verse 5, *"Persia"* and then *"Cush"* and *"Put."* (In the King James Version you will not read it that way but rather you will read it "Ethiopia" and "Libya"). In the case of the latter two names the King James Version is correct in its interpretation.

What is this *"Persia"* referred to here? At the time that Ezekiel wrote this prophecy, Cyrus the Great had not yet conquered Persia. So Ezekiel referred to those nations, peoples and tribes known as the Aryans who inhabited what is called today Armenian Russia, the northern part of Iraq, and also the northern part of what today is called Iran. We cannot, therefore, definitely say that this prophecy refers to Persia or Iran as we know it today. It may; it may not. We do not know.

GOMER. In verse six, *"Gomer, and all his hordes;"* (in the King James it says "bands," but it means the traveling bands of men, soldiers). "Gomer" was another immediate descendant of Noah and his descendants who settled to the north of the Black Sea in what is today called the Soviet Union. The inhabitants of that area then moved westward into what is today known as Germany. The implication I think is very clear that at least East Germany is included within the scope of this prophecy.

This reference is to *eastern* Germany and Poland. Gibbon *(Decline and Fall of the Roman Empire)* says the *German* detachment of *Gomer* marched under the banner of Ashkenaz, the son of Gomer. (Vol. 1, p. 204). Gibbon was referring to the conquest of what is now Poland, part of Russia and East Germany in the generations following Noah's flood. Ashkenaz was the great grandson of Noah.

Jews from Germany, Russia and Poland are commonly referred to, even now, as "ASHKENAZIM." Proof of this is plentiful.

(1) *The Encyclopaedia Brittanica* (Vol. 10, p. 511) says Gomer represents the people known as the CIMMERIANS and originated in the district north of the Black Sea, i.e., Russia. Of course, they spread westward into Germany by the time of Ezekiel. We must think of their location at Ezekiel's time, not later, as we read his prediction, but it certainly means East Germany today.

(2) *Herodotus,* the famed "Father of history," said in his account of Scythia that the Cimmerians inhabited South Russia. From there it is obvious they went north towards Germany, as the centuries passed.

(3) *Josephus,* the great first century historian, called the sons of Ashkenaz, "the Rheginians" and a map of the ancient Roman Empire places them in the area of Czechoslovakia and Germany.

(4) *The Talmud,* the Jewish commentary of ancient times, flatly states that the sons of Gomer were the Germans,

in the sense that the tribes of Gomer and his descendants eventually followed the Danube River from Russia into Germany.

TOGARMAH. Ezekiel also mentions another nation, *"the house of Togarmah of the north quarters."* Ezekiel was writing in Babylon and the next country north is what we call Asia Minor, divided today among Turkey, Iran, Iraq and the Soviet Union. Ezekiel most specifically refers to these people as, "of the north quarters," thus pushing again the prophecy up to include another portion of the Soviet Union in terms of the geographical occupation of the tribe of Togarmah in that day.

Togarmah was the second son of Gomer, and his descendants occupied northern and eastern Turkey, and Turkestan, which is now part of the Soviet Union. The prophecy of Ezekiel speaks of "Togarmah and all his bands (tribes)," so we are safe in looking toward the southern part of the Soviet Union which in other days was composed of many small nations such as Armenia and including some of the Tartar hordes who lived in Asia south of the Sea of Aral and between that sea and the Caspian Sea.

Dr. Raymond Edman, the late President of Wheaton College, affirmed:

> "The ancestors of modern Armenia claim that the father of their race, HAIK, was the son of Togarmah." (Sunday School Times, quoted by Bauman).

Dr. Harry Rimmer wrote:

> "Togarmah has always been the land we call Armenia," i.e., a part of the Soviet Union. *(The Coming War and the Rise of Russia,* p. 62)

So all these countries, named by Ezekiel by the names with which he was familiar in 570 B.C., are to be linked in a terrible invasion army. The scope of it ranges from Africa to Asiatic Siberia; from Germany to the Balkans, from Moscow to many

Arab nations in the Middle East and in Africa, along the southern coast of the Mediterranean. Think of it — all these bloody Communist nations, uninhibited by Christian tradition, converging on the land of Israel and her neighbors! *Gog,* the leader, comes from the *north,* but his allies come from every direction of the compass. The invasion group consists of the Huns, the Mongol hordes, the Cossacks, some Arabs, the Africans and the Russians, all moving toward the land-bridge of three continents, toward the land of Israel, and that of her immediate neighbors! Though this war is geographically focused, it is a *world* war. Perhaps it will even be called, "World War III."

Other Nations Mentioned by Ezekiel Who Will Oppose Russia

Ezekiel in 38:13,18, lists the nations who will oppose the great 'northern' confederacy. He used the ancient names of these nations as we have said. Who are they?

ISRAEL. This is the Israel gathered out of the dispersion which is filled with those who have re-established their ancient country, "who dwell safely in unwalled villages." There is no mistake about the main objective of the Soviet confederacy: it is Israel. However, we would be greatly mistaken to identify this by the boundaries of modern Israel. Part of ancient Israel is located in Jordan, which speaks of the location of the battle as to be in the "valley of the passengers on the east of the sea." The "sea" is Galilee, and the "valley of the passengers" is probably the valley lying to the east of the sea, well within modern Jordanian territory. It also continues east of the Dead Sea southwards. Interestingly, Dr. Taylor, in his paraphrase of this passage translates it as "the Dead Sea."

SHEBA. The queen of Sheba who visited King Solomon probably came from the south of Arabia, perhaps in the area of the oil rich countries of the southwestern edge of the Arabian peninsula. (See Schaff-Hertsog Encyclopaedia, p. 249). Archaeologists have confirmed this, notably W. F. Albright and Wendell Phillips in their expedition there conducted in 1947.

DEDAN. Davis' *Dictionary of the Bible* identifies this nation as the Arabs of the northern part of the Arabian desert, notably in Saudi Arabia today. It is also very instructive that Saudi Arabia has refused to accept Arab socialism, but instead so far remains loyal to the free world. Startingly, the ancient capitol of Saudi Arabia is still called *Dedan* on the maps today!

JORDAN. Though the bitterness between modern Israel and Jordan remains acute, it is notable that it is less violent than the hatred of Syria against Israel and vice versa. Pressure from the Arab world is upon the Hashemite Kingdom of the Jordan to resist any settlement with Israel which would legitimatize Israel as a nation. However the recent history-making visit of President Sadat of Egypt to Israel may mark the beginning of an alliance against Russia which *must* come someday if not soon!

The writer, who has journeyed 35 times throughout most of the Middle East, offers an opinion that Jordan and Israel are, despite their quarrels, *natural* allies, and if it were not for the pressure upon Jordan from the rest of the Arab world, *peace* could be worked out even now to the complete satisfaction of both nations. Jordan is a fine nation, and every real Christian in the world wishes it well and has a kindly attitude toward it. Jordan and Israel, as sacred lands, are both dear to the hearts of almost all people in the United States, and these two nations would be instantly defended by the United States in case either of them were threatened seriously by others. At least, such is the present reality. Further, it would behoove both Israel and Jordan to look well into Ezekiel's prophecy, since the common threat of Communism will some day unite them to some degree, whether or not they can believe this at the moment. War makes strange bedfellows, and as surely as the Bible is true, these two nations will some day unite their intentions to oppose the Russian horde.

It is interesting to note in one of the phophecies concerning the Northern Confederacy that the area now known as *Jordan* is mentioned by name. There is a whole passage in Daniel given to the same events as those Ezekiel saw. In this passage "Gog" is called the "King of the North," and it is predicted that he will enter (invade) into "The glorious land" (The Holy Land).

> "He shall enter also into the glorious land, and many countries shall be overthrown: but these escape out of His hand, even Edom, and Moab, and the chief of the children of Ammon." — Daniel 11:41

The present boundaries of Jordan encompass the countries of Edom, Moab and the land of Ammon. Today Jordan has Amman (ancient Rabath-Ammon) as her capital city. You will note that in Ezekiel's vision the Arabian nations including Dedan and Sheba (Dedan as we have noted is another ancient name for Saudi Arabia) are to challenge the Soviet Confederacy. *Daniel* is even more specific. He says Jordan will escape. Daniel notes also that Ethiopia and Libya will be allied with Russia. The two prophecies of Daniel and Ezekiel *fit each other* with beautiful precision!

Now, we return to Ezekiel's prophecy for the identity of the last of the challengers of the Soviet invaders.

The Merchants of Tarshish and All the Young Lions Thereof

Of all the groups and nations mentioned in Ezekiel, this is the hardest to identify. Attempts have been made to identify "Tarshish" with "Tarsus" in Turkey. If this were so, the whole prophecy would be so confused as to be meaningless. Certainly today there is no significance to Turkey as a world power. Were Turkey to be the only ally Israel, Sheba and Dedan had, since these few Jewish and Arab peoples are not strong themselves (though they do have the advantage of being *on the ground* which is to be invaded) there would be little resistance indeed to the Soviet advance. And, in any case, *Tarsus* was never mentioned as standing for Turkey as a whole in ancient literature.

Davis in his *Dictionary of the Bible* (p. 723) concerning Tarshish asserts:

> "It was a distant land (Is. 66:19) . . . It is believed that Tarshish was Tartessus, in the south of Spain, near Gibraltar (Herod LV. 152) . . . Ships of Tarshish were originally ships trading to and from Tarshish, but ultimately ships of first-rate magnitude to whatever place their voyages may have been made."

We shall demonstrate that this identification is correct.

Who Were the Merchants of Tarshish?

Only in the past half dozen years has much light been thrown on the historic location of ancient Tarshish. Books and articles in learned archaeological journals written before that time now seem to have rather limited value. In some instances they are more confusing than helpful, despite the prestige of their authors. The reasons for certainty of identification are found in the recent discoveries of archaeology and the confirmation that ancient authorities were right all along in their identification of Tarshish as a Western European colonizing power based in Spain.

Sardinia

The justly famous archaeologist, William F. Albright, for example, was convinced that Tarshish was located on the island of Sardinia. This despite the clear indications, even from ancient Roman writers, to the effect that Tarshish was founded some time just after the Trojan War (1109 B.C.) in western Spain near the present city of Cadiz. Commenting on such ideas that the Phoenicians were limited in their westward outreach, the noted scholar of the Phoenicians, Moscoti, says:

> In recent times flaws have been found in this attitude. Even archaeologists are beginning to place Phoenician expansion in the Mediterranean at an earlier period. They claim that lack of evidence is no argument and refer to the information contained in archaeological findings and in inscriptions which have so far been neglected. — (Sabatino Moscoti, *The World of the Phoenicians*, p. 95)

> Furthermore, at the time of Solomon, the Bible mentions the merchant fleet of Tyre, capable of undertaking long and difficult crossings. It mentions specifically a "navy of Tarshish," and, in all likelihood, Tarshish must be identified with the southwestern area of Spain.

This is the probable location of ancient Tarshish, near Cadiz, Spain.

Now, it is quite possible that in this case the expression may mean 'ocean-going navy,' but nevertheless the reference exists and so, since we have no reason to doubt the veracity of Biblical sources in this respect, it seems probable that Phoenician navigators had penetrated to the far West as early as the tenth century and obviously had to make use of numerous landing-stages. — (Moscoti, p. 96-97)

. . . it must be kept in mind that the Phoenicians did not only settle in places where colonies subsequently developed but also founded trading-posts in regions ethnically and politically different, and either remained there as small settlements or dissolved. — (Moscoti, p. 97-98)

Proceding farther along the African coast of the Mediterranean, the earliest colony, traditionally, is Utica. Velleius Paterculus says that the Phoenician fleet which controlled the seas founded Cadiz about eighty years after the fall of Troy and Utica a little later. Since he ascribes the fall of Troy elsewhere to c. 1190 B.C., Cadiz appears to have been founded c. 1110 and Utica c. 1100. — (Moscoti, p. 98-99)

Tarshish

Perhaps we have enough information now to clear up much of the mystery of what and where Tarshish was. Moscoti has set out the opinion that "Tarshish" at first, was a reference to *Tarsus* in Asia Minor, and the same name was later given to *Tartessus* in Spain because of the similarity of the consonants in the name itself.

Perhaps this may have originally been the case. But from at least 1010 B.C., it is clear that the Phoenicians were in western Spain beyond Gibraltar at the place the Romans called *Gades* and which today is known as Cadiz. The colonial trading post of Tarshish (which came to be its name) was located not far away at the mouth of the Guadalquivir River in southwestern Spain. Moscoti seems certain about this and observes:

"Finally, the most controversial point about Phoenician colonization concerns Spain. The colony of Cadiz goes back traditionally to the end of the twelfth century. The material from it is far later (fifth century) and the earlier remains of other localities, which can probably be ascribed to the eight century, are still far from the traditional date. Tarshish (Tartessus) was probably to the north of Cadiz, at the source of the Guadalquivir. The most likely opinions place it on the site of Asta Regia. The identification of Tarshish with Tartessus leads us to believe that we can ascribe Phoenician settlement in Spain to the tenth century, if not to the traditional date. Another reason for earlier ascriptions of the archaeological data is provided by Mazar's mission in Spain in 1957, the results of which have not yet been published. Mazar asserts that there are archaeological traces of the Phoenicians in Spain going back at least as far as the ninth century." — (Moscoti, p. 100)

The German writer, Gerhard Herm, also traces Tarshish in much the same way:

"The routes which the Carthaginian ships followed were essentially the same as those which the East Phoenicians had chosen. Above all, they linked Tartessus, the land rich in minerals, to the colonized countries of the east, including Greece. But where was Tartessus?

"One can only say with certainty that this mysterious place was an area in southern Spain. Strabo thought it was a river 'with springs rich in silver,' whereas Herodotus told of a king who ruled over Tartessus, and so must have thought it was a country. If one pieces together everything which the classical authors wrote about it, one gets the picture of a large community which took its name from a river, the present-day Guadalquivir, and which lay on an island between the two arms of its estuary. It was rich, because the river came from the 'silver mountains' and brought great quantities of the different noble and non-ferrous metals with it. Especially tin, copper, gold and silver.

"If this description is approximately accurate, the Iberian El Dorado must have been situated near the sherry town of Jerez de la Frontera, *between the Guadalquivir and the Rio Guadalete,* because the first of these two rivers does not have two mouths. The silver mountains, however, were identical with the Sierra Morena, a mountain range in which there are in fact rich deposits of copper and also smaller quantities

of silver and gold. But there is, at any rate now, no tin there."
— (Gerhard Herm, *The Phoenicians*, p. 204)

It is evident that the city of Tarshish, as such, ceased to exist sometime around the *end* of the lifetime of Ezekiel. Nevertheless, as Herm explains, the "merchants of Tarshish" continued to trade and flourish from their better port of Cadiz.

"In 500 B.C. Tartessus disappeared from sight so mysteriously that Plato was inspired — or so one imagines — to base his Atlantis myth on it. The facts which remain are: from their old base of Cadiz (which lies opposite the mouth of the Rio Guadalete) the Carthaginians traded with an Iberian people, who must already have had skilled miners, and then transported the ore back to the Mediterranean. In addition, they appear to have also bought or occupied land there, because an old chronicle, based on Greek texts, the *De ora maritima* of the Latin poet Avienus, speaks of many 'peoples and towns,' beyond the Pillars of Hercules, which were ruled by the Carthaginians. Modern historians have even suggested that more than twenty ports of varying sizes on the Atlantic coast of Spain and Portugal owe their origins to West Phoenician activities and that the North African town ruled almost half of Spain. The limits of the Carthaginian sphere of influence are generally indicated today by a line from the mouth of the Ebro to that of the Tagus. Hannibal later advanced as far as Helmantike, present-day Salamanca. Carthgena (New Carthage), Saguntum and possibly Malaga were built by his countrymen."

Herm raises the intriguing possibility that some Jews may have sailed on the ships of Tarshish.

"Among other things, these and later settlements in Iberia gave rise to a strange rumor, which claims that the many Spanish Jews who, until their banishment in the late fifteenth century had played such an important and splendid role in the commercial and spiritual life of the Christian territory between Gibraltar and the Pyrenees, were in fact genuine descendants of the Phoenicians, whom they so much resembled. To support this thesis, it is claimed that their great number — around the year 1490 there were in Spain more than 300,000 Jews — cannot even be explained by assuming that large numbers of them immigrated together with the Moors.

And further. so say the suporters of this theory, after the Reconquista. no one could really tell the difference between Semitic-looking people of Jewish, Islamic or Christian belief. Whoever looked like a Jew or a "Marrano" (literally: pig), a baptized Jew was considered to be one. And since the Phoenicians or their descendants were not very different from genuine Jews or their descendants. the suspicion gains in probability that there were perhaps many, many great-grand-nephews of Carthaginian merchants among the Sephardim who were banished by the Grand Inquisitor Troquemada to North Africa, Turkey or to South America and who there established their impressive money dynasties." — (Herm, p. 205-206)

Tartessus

The most famous trading or merchant nation in the Middle East in the thousand years before Christ was that of the Phoe-

Ancient fortress on the sea in Cadiz, Spain, founded by the Phoenicians.

25

nicians. Because *Tartessus* became their famed outpost, the name, as we have seen, was somehow changed to *"Tarshish."* The entire Western trading fleet, it has been determined, was referred to as "The Ships of Tarshish," and the Phoenicians who traveled through the Mediterranean beyond Gibraltar were called "The Merchants of Tarshish." Moscoti writes:

"We now come to one of the main problems of Phoenician colonial expansion: the problem of Tarshish-Tartessus, from which an entire aspect of the movement of Mediterranean expansion depends. Starting with the Biblical source, we read with reference to Solomon that 'the king had at sea a navy of Tarshish with the navy of Hiram: once in three years came the navy of Tarshish, bringing gold and silver, ivory, apes and peacocks.' Jeremiah mentions Tarshish and gold from Ophir. Ezekiel tells Tyre: 'Tarshish was thy merchant by reason of the multitude of all kind of riches; with silver, iron, tin and lead, they traded in thy fairs.' From these quotations and others of less importance, it seems clear that, even if 'navy of Tarshish' can generically mean (ocean-going navy,) the expression originates from the fact that *Tarshish* designates a city or a region in the West, particularly rich in metals. The epoch to which the texts refer can be placed around the tenth century and after it.

"Passing on to the classical sources, it is obvious that Tartessus is a locality in southern Spain. The poet Stesichorus, who wrote c. 600 B.C. in Sicily, has left us a line quoted by Strabo which mentions 'the unlimited, silver-rooted springs of the river Tartessus.' If this refers to the river, the city is mentioned by the poet Anacreon (c. 530) again quoted by Strabo, with reference to Arganthonius, long-lived king of Tartessus. In the fifth century, but referring to an earlier period, Herodotus tells of the voyage of Kolaios to Tartessus, and of the friendship between the Phoenicians and the local king Arganthonius."

Finally, from various authors of the sixth century, the following description of Tartessus was reconstructed:

"Tartessus is an illustrious city of Iberia which takes its name from the river Baetis (Guadalquivir) formerly also called Tartessus. This river comes from the Celtic region and has its source in the 'silver mountain'; in its stream it carries, besides silver and tin, a great abundance of gold and bronze. The river Tartessus divides into two arms when it reaches the mouth. Tartessus, the city, stands between the two arms, as on an island."

"Now, is the Biblical Tarshish definitely the same as the Greek Tartessus? Recent studies tend to give Tarshish a common rather than a proper value, meaning 'mine' (from the Semetic root *rss*). If this hypothesis is not very probable, we must also mention the fact that Tarshish appears in the genealogy of Genesis, together with Elisha and Kittim, both names indicating the island of Cyprus, which would validate the ancient theory, sustained by Josephus and Eusebius, that Tarshish is to be identified with Tarsus in Cilicia. Whatever the value of these observations, however, it seems certain that at a given moment Tarshish really was taken to denote Tartessus, evidently because of the phonetic affinity.

"Tartessus, therefore, was a city and state which extended far and was rich from the trade in metals. What was its relationship with Cadiz? It seems likely that the Phoenicians of Cadiz succeeded to the Tartessian routes and trade, or in any case used and supported them. And this is why the Phoenicians founded Cadiz in the neighbourhood of Tartessus. But where exactly was Tartessus? The traditional Spanish theory places the town on the site of Messas de Asta, *ancient Asta Regia,* near Jerez. Others have sought it at Donnana, at the mouth of the Guadalquivir, but excavations have not confirmed this theory. A further possible hypothesis places it in Huelva or in the neighbourhood, on the island of Saltes. In any case, the ancient city, the remains of which have not definitely been identified by archaeology, was in the region of the lower Guadalquivir." — (Moscoti, p. 231-232)

There was a good reason for the location of Tarshish. It was the Atlantic coast point of trans-shipment for all goods sent from the places where the Phoenicians picked them up. For a typical example, if they received trading items from Egypt or Israel, they would carry them to Tarshish. There they would be sent via another ship to, say, Britain, where they would load British minerals, such as tin, lead, or silver in exchange.

These ships in turn would be sent back to Tarshish and offloaded. Another vessel would then take these valuable minerals on to Egypt or *Israel,* or perhaps even to some other Mediterranean port. Since Tarshish was, until the mercantile operation was later moved to the safer and more commodious port of Cadiz, the chief early trading settlement bearing the name, "Tarshish," the name stayed. The actual original trading post itself probably was abandoned. No trace of it has so far been found, though the presence of the same Phoenician traders in Cadiz from the time of King David (1000 B.C.) is well established in and around Cadiz in Spain and from that time until the present. To all that has been said we can add the testimony of Wiseman.

> "Traditionally, the earliest settlement in the west was at Gades (Cadiz) on the Atlantic coast of Southern Spain, founded in the twelfth century on what was then a small islet at the mouth of the Guadalete, an excellent spot from which to ship the ores mined at Spanish Tarshish or Tartessus, some miles inland." — (Wiseman, p. 280)

Moscoti tells of the purposes of the "Merchants of Tarshish."

> "The Phoenicians colonized Spain in order to obtain control of the sources of the metal trade (gold, tin and above all, silver), which they later sold in the East at a large profit. The ancient authors tell us of this, and Diodorus, insisting on the essential value of this traffic, leads us to believe that it was the reason for, rather than the result of, the foundation of the colonies.

> "And the result was that the Phoenicians, as in the course of many years they prospered greatly thanks to commerce of this kind, sent forth many colonies, some to Sicily and its neighbouring islands, and others to Libya, Sardinia and Iberia.

> "We have a series of accounts concerning the period of the colonization of Cadiz. Strabo, quoting Posidonius, tells that various expeditions were sent by the Tyrians to the Pillars of Hercules, and that the third of these expeditions resulted in the foundation of Cadiz with the sanctuary on the eastern part of the island and the city on the western part. Valleius Paterculus specifies that eighty years after the fall of Troy,

c. 1110, the Tyrian fleet, which ruled the sea, founded Cadiz at the tip of Spain on an island surrounded by the Ocean and separated from the mainland by a short strait; soon after, adds, the same Tyrians founded Utica. Since the sources of Utica provide the date of 1101, nothing seems to contradict the founding of Cadiz in 1110." —— (Moscoti, p. 230)

"Cadiz was in a very important position, from the commercial point of view, since it guarded the area of the silver-mines of Tartessus. It was, therefore, evidently one of the first Phoenician settlements, and the tradition according to which Lixus, on the Moroccan coast, was founded before Cadiz (as Pliny says) is also significant. From these cities, the Phoenicians could control the Mediterranean trade routes and at the same time open the routes on the Atlantic coasts (of Europe)." — (Moscoti, p. 231)

Herm agrees that the trading colonies of Tarshish included ports in Great Britain.

"The suffetes seem therefore to have known very well what their monopoly on the British tin trade was worth, and this in turn would indicate that such a trade did exist. It is known that the coveted metal from Britain had already reached the Continent in the Bronze Age and that the Tartessians played a part in obtaining it." — (Herm, p. 206)

Cadiz

By the time Ezekiel wrote, the "Merchants (i.e. traders *by sea)* of Tarshish" generally operated out of Cadiz and established trading posts which had grown into sizeable colonies, up the entire coasts of Western Europe to and including Britain.

"At first there was no need for colonies to be numerous, since it was only possible to control navigation in certain points. This assumption of the Atlantic strongholds was obvious to the ancient historians: Strabo claims that after the Trojan War the Phoenicians sailed beyond the Pillars of Hercules and founded cities there." — (Moscoti, p. 231A)

Historians are indebted to the very intimate knowledge Ezekiel had of the exact nature of the Tarshish merchant marine and its typical items of trade. Most of the histories of the Phoenicians gladly quote the detailed description Ezekiel gives, which indicates a very thorough knowledge on his part before he became a captive in Babylon. Doubtless Ezekiel had visited Tyre and Sidon and had seen the Tarshish ships for himself.

So Ezekiel later wrote this description:

"O Tyre, thou hast said, I am of perfect beauty. Thy borders are in the midst of the seas, thy builders have perfected thy beauty. They have made all thy ship boards of fir trees of Senir: they have taken cedars from Lebanon to make masts for thee. Of the oaks of Bashan have they made thine oars; the company of Ashurites have made thy benches of ivory, brought of the isles of Chittim. Fine linen with broidered work from Egypt was that which thou spreadest forth to be thy sail; blue and purple from the isles of Elishash was that which covered thee. The inhabitants of Sidon and Aradus were thy mariners: thy wise men, O Tyre, that were in thee, were thy pilots. The ancients of Gebal and the wise men thereof were in thee thy calkers: all the ships of the sea with their mariners were in thee to occupy thy merchandise. They of Persia and of Lud and of Phut were in thine army, thy men of war: they hanged the shield and helmet in thee; they set forth thy comeliness. The men of Aradus with thine army were upon thy walls round about, and the Gammadims were in thy towers; they hanged their shields upon thy walls round about; they have made thy beauty perfect. Tarshish was thy merchant by reason of the multitude of all kind of riches; with silver, iron, tin, and lead they traded in thy fairs. Javan, Tubal, and Meshech, were thy merchants: they traded the persons of men and vessels of brass in thy market. They of the house of Togarmah traded in thy fairs with horses and horsemen and mules. The men of Dedan were thy merchants; many isles were the merchandise of thine hand: they brought thee for a present horns of ivory and ebony. Syria was thy merchant by reason of the multitude of the wares of thy making: they occupied in thy fairs with emeralds, purple, and broidered work, and fine linen, and coral, and agate. Judah, and the land of Israel, they were thy merchants: they traded in thy market wheat of Minnith, and Pannag, and honey, and oil, and balm. Damascus was thy merchant in the multitude of the wares of thy making, for the multitude of all riches; in the wind of Helbon, and white wool, Dan also and Javan going to and fro occupied in thy fairs: bright iron, cassia, and calamus were in thy market. Dedan was thy merchant in precious clothes for chariots.

"Arabia, and all the princes of Kedar, they occupied with thee, in lambs, and in rams, and goats: in these were they thy merchants. The merchants of Sheba and Raamah, they were thy merchants: they occupied in thy fairs with chief of all spices, and with all precious stones and gold. Haran, and Canneh and Eden the merchants of Sheba, Asshur, and Chilmad were thy merchants. These were thy merchants in all sorts of things, in blue clothes, and broidered work, and in chests of rich apparel, bound with cords, and made of cedar, among thy merchandise. The ships of Tarshish did sing of thee in thy market: and thou wast replenished, and made very glorious in the midst of the seas." — (Ezekiel 27:3-25)

Moscoti explains the historical value of Ezekiel's knowledge of the Phoenician traders and locates some of the places of trade by the Merchants of Tarshish who, of course, had originally come from Tyre.

"In the first part of the passage, the allegorical image of Tyre as a great ship suggests the goods she traded by mentioning the materials used to build the ship, and the people taken as sailors. The wood implies Mount Hermon (of which Senir is a peak), the Lebanon, Bashan (north-east of Lake Tiberias) and Cyprus (Chittim, from the name of the Phoenician colony Kition)." — (Moscoti, pp. 84-85)

What Did the "Merchants of Tarshish" Mean to Ezekiel?

We must not assume that the prophets always understood visions given to them. Daniel certainly did not (see Dan. Chapter 12). Ezekiel foresaw, but perhaps did not fully understand the distant time when all Israel (not merely Judah which was then in captivity in Babylon) would be gathered out of the nations of the whole world, where they had been scattered, and restored to their own land. It is not our purpose here to identify just who came to constitute "Israel" in captivity. Certainly Judah eventually became the main rallying force for all Israel in exile.

But a fully representative return of Israel from many nations never happened, not even in the return of the 25,000 Judeans from Babylon under Ezra, that is, until the twentieth century of our era. So we cannot attribute the prophecy about this in the 38th chapter to a slightly later time and authorship than that of Ezekiel, by suggesting that some other writer actually experienced the events and then claimed his forged prophecy was made by Ezekiel himself.

Plainly, Ezekiel himself saw the return of Israel from the many nations where the people of Israel were scattered. Isaiah says they will return in "ships of Tarshish." (Isa. 60:9) *Who* did Ezekiel and Isaiah mean by this description which has been so long and so unnecessarily considered enigmatic? Surely the "ships of Tarshish," as envisioned by Isaiah must be identifiable in the days of the return. *Who are they?*

There is no reason to doubt that both prophets saw, or meant, the nations which were colonized by the Phoenicians of Tarshish. It was the Phoenician merchants who traded with and established colonies in those nations, as we have abundantly proven in the lengthy quotations from scholars who specialize in Phoenician history. The only sea-link (from 1000 B.C. to 100 B.C.) between Britain and France, or Spain, or Rome for that matter, came from the actual ships of Tarshish based at first in Tarshish and later in Cadiz. So when Ezekiel mentions the Merchants of Tarshish he is referring to lands first colonized by the Phoenicians, later to be called by other names.

If further proof of the Phoenician colonies being meant by Ezekiel, hear again from Moscoti:

"Beyond the Pillars of Hercules, on the Atlantic coast, new centers undoubtedly radiated from ancient Cadiz. The *Ora Maritima of Avienus*, in a translation from a Greek text datable soon after 500, says that the Carthaginians 'had peoples and cities' beyond the Pillars of Hercules, and the Periplus of Pseudo-Skylaz in the fourth century mentions many Carthaginian trading-posts in the region . . .

"That Carthaginian penetration was not restricted to the coastal settlements, but spread a certain distance inland in the southern region, and that it was accompanied by ethnic infiltrations is proved by the repeated reference to 'Liby-phoenicians' in the classical sources as the population of the area in question. They were evidently Carthaginian settlers in whom the North African element played a strong part; but the term only applies to this particular zone and does not extend to Cadiz and the Atlantic coast on one side nor to Ibiza on the other." — (Moscoti, p. 234)

It was said that so busy were the Tarshish mercantile ships in 500 B.C. that in Cadiz a person need wait only an average of three days and he could get passage on a ship going to just about any port in the Mediterranean or Western Europe.

"There was so much maritime traffic that within 3 days a traveler could find a ship to take him any place he fancied in the Mediterranean." — (Herm, p. 236)

The "Young Lions" of Tarshish

This phrase carries Ezekiel's identification of the nations which shall protest or challenge the Russian-led confederacy as it invades Israel, to a further, more logical, more certain identification. "Young lions" is, in the Hebrew, "whelps" or "cubs"; obviously, offsprings or colonies. The "Merchants of Tarshish" were definitely colonizers. This is the plain and logical meaning of the phrase Ezekiel used.

After all, what else could he say if the mysterious vision was for a future time? He *must* perforce have used the terms and names of his own day. He probably did not understand the full implication of what he wrote. But he surely would say that long after his time, a new confederacy of power would arise from the western Atlantic nations, whose armies, riches and power might also provide the means of a future role in the preservation of Israel.

Why should we assume the ancient writers, such as Ezekiel, knew little about European areas which we know sprung into full historical life quite early? In 70 B.C. Caesar conquered Gaul, which he recorded as already having founded great cities. This was long before the time of Christ. Several early Caesars came from Spain, notably Hadrian. How did Spain produce such men in the first century if the land of Spain were not fully civilized long before their time?

Our own concepts of the ancient world are themselves almost provincial and mythological. If Solomon could trade with Britain via the "Merchants of Tarshish" (in 950 B.C.) why do we suppose that the location of Tarshish was unknown to Ezekiel in 550 B.C., or that its location and activities were mere folk tales? We are the ignorant ones if we assume that because in the Middle Ages ships were very small and distant ports unreachable that the same conditions prevailed before then in the thousand years before Christ.

In matter of fact, before the time of Jesus, there existed sea-going vessels of a vastly larger size and better sea-worthiness than those Columbus used in his voyages supposedly to India, which instead accidentally resulted in the "discovery" of America. Herm deals with this:

> "We know less about the Carthaginian merchant ships than about these warships, but they must have also been fairly large. At all events, they were larger than the boats in which the English settlers went to America in the seventeenth century. The *Mayflower* had a displacement of 180 tons, whereas Roman corn freighters in the third century B.C. carried well over a thousand tons, and the Carthaginian ships cannot have been much smaller." — (Herm, p. 202)

Wiseman also furnishes proof of the size and capacity of the Tarshish ships:

"There is reference to Phoenician maritime enterprise on the Palermo Stone inscription (c. 2200 B.C.) of forty timber-carrying ships from Byblos, and suggests that, by this time, commercial sea-going traffic had long been established; in fact, alabaster vases bearing Egyptian royal cartouches of the Second Dynasty have been found in Byblos. Nor were these Fourth Dynasty ships mere boats; the Palermo Stone reveals that the wood carried was for the construction of three ships each 170 feet long. The actual ship which was built of Phoenician cedar for Khufu, the Cheops of pyramid fame who followed Shefru, was found in 1954. The wood was probably exported from Byblos, which seems to have been the earliest of the Phoenician cities to have developed and, from early dynastic times, to have had very close links with Egypt." — (Wiseman, *Peoples of Old Testament Times*, pp. 264-265)

Modern trading "ships of Tarshish" docked for loading goods. Ancient Tarshish ships were even larger. This photo shows the use of loading ships in one of the world's oldest ports, near Cadiz, Spain.

"Phoenician sailing expertise is well indicated by the feat whereby at the command of pharaoh Necho, they circumnavigated the whole of Africa c. 600 B.C., traveling three years for the voyage. Later, (c. 450) sailors from the Tyrian colony of Carthage sailed as far as Britain under admiral Hamilco, probably testing the practicability of a sea route to come by Cornish tin. A little later again, Hanno sailed from Carthage down the west coast of Africa, maybe as far as the Niger, and when he got back he wrote an account of his voyage which was inscribed in the temple of Ba'al Hammon. A somewhat garbled Greek version is still extant. Madeira and the Azores may have been discovered by accident, but the alleged discovery of an authentic Phoenician inscription at Paraibo in Brazil is still regarded with skepticism." — (Wiseman, p. 277-78)

Herm raises the theory that the colonies of the Tarshish merchants may have included some in the Americas.

"Before doing so, they (the Phoenicians) would have passed through the Straits of Gibraltar, and seen that beyond it stretched another endless ocean, far more stormy than the one they knew, and moved by tides. This was a phenomenon which also amazed Alexander the Great in India centuries later. There were no tides in the Mediterranean. How the Phoenicians reacted is not recorded. They appear to have simply grown accustomed to the fact and were soon feeling their way down the Atlantic coast of Africa. According to as yet unconfirmed theories, they then even veered westwards and sailed as far as America. Professor Cyrus H. Gordon of Brandeis University in Boston, at any rate, put forward the supposition that the Melungeons, a light-skinned Indian tribe in East Tennessee came, as they themselves believe, from Phoenicia. Two and a half millennia before Columbus, these ancestors of theirs landed on the shores of the New World and became settlers there. Anyone who has studied the Tyrians and their voyages for any length of time will be inclined to think that this theory is likely. They were an amazing people. The things they have not recounted would fill at least as many volumes as all that the Greeks have told so volubly." — (Herm, p. 137-8)

Perhaps when Herm did his research the amazing discoveries of Professor Barry Fell of Harvard were not yet published. But in 1976, Fell's book, *America B.C.,* (which was the basis of the lead article in the February 1977 Reader's Digest) settled once and for all the fact that the colonies of Tarshish included many in what is now the United States!

The Astonishing Discoveries of Professor Fell

Perhaps one of the most important archaeological finds made public in recent years which have a bearing on the identity of the nations in Ezekiel's prophecy in chapters 38 and 39 has come to full disclosure in a book by Professor Barry Fell, called *"America B.C."* This very scholarly and highly technical volume records a multitude of discoveries which prove that the many hitherto mysterious inscriptions discovered in the Americas are actually traceable to a thousand years of commerce by sea between Tarshish in Spain and the various Phoenician colonies in *what is now the United States.* The reader is urged to obtain and study for himself these proofs of the history of the ancient settlers in the new world. Dr. Fell tells of them in terms of a very busy commercial colonization and trade, as follows:

"In the wake of the Celtic pioneers came the Phoenician traders of Spain, men from Cadiz who spoke the punic tongue, but wrote it in the peculiar style of lettering known as Iberian script. Although some of these traders seem to have settled only on the coast, and then only temporarily, leaving a few engraved stones to mark their visits or record their claims of territorial annexation, other Phoenicians remained here and, together with Egyptian miners, became part of the Wabanaki tribe of New England. Further south, Basque sailors came to Pennsylvania and established a temporary settlement there, leaving however no substantial monuments other than grave markers bearing their names. Further south still, Libyan and Egyptian mariners entered the Mississippi from the Gulf of Mexico, penetrating inland to Iowa and the Dakotas, and westward along the Arkansas and Cimarron Rivers, to leave behind inscribed records of their presence. Norse and Basque visitors reached the Gulf of St. Lawrence, introducing various mariner's terms into the language of the northern Algonquian Indians. Descendants of these visitors are also to be found apparently among the Amerindian tribes, several of which employ dialects derived in part from the ancient tongues of Phoenicia and North Africa." — (America B.C., p. 7)

One of Fell's most thrilling discoveries, as it bears upon this study is that of inscriptions which mention Tarshish by name. In his chapter entitled "Ships of Tarshish," Fell observes:

"By the eight century B.C. a group of Syrian colonists had settled the lower reaches of the valley of the Guadalquivir River in Andalusia, southwestern Spain, where they were engaged in trading for metals mined by the natives, who seem to have been mainly Basques. Eventually invading bands of Celts in ever-increasing numbers came down from the north, and by 500 B.C. they had overrun the whole region. Thereafter we hear no more of Phoenicians in this part of Andalusia. Now, however, we have found their inscriptions in America.

"The alphabet has been deciphered in part by Spanish epigraphers, and most of the residual letters have now been assigned their phonetic values as a result of the discovery of Tartessian inscriptions in Central and North America. The language can now be read with relative ease, for it proves to be no more than a dialectal variant of Phoenician. In fact, one wonders why the Tartessians bothered to devise their own script, seeing they could equally well have employed the script of Phoenicia itself.

"From the Bible we learn that the ships of Tarshish were the largest seagoing vessels known to the Semitic world, and the name was eventually applied to any large ocean-going vessel. On the coasts of Palestine, where the ancient psalmists of Israel could watch the vessels of their Phoenician cousins plying their trade with Lebanon and Egypt, the ships of Tarshish became proverbial as an expression of sea power.

"Tarshish was ruled by kings, as we learn from Psalm 72, kings of comparable power to those who ruled over Sheba, since both are mentioned in the same breath, and grouped with the princes of the isles, by which is probably meant the Phoenician kings of Cyprus and Sardinia.

"Tartessian vessels would surely have played a major role in the Celtic migration to New England." — (America B.C., p. 93)

The finding of the Tarshish inscription itself is related by Dr. Fell:

"It was not until 1975 that Pearson's original unretouched photograph came to my notice through the courtesy of James Whittall. Some months later at Union, New Hampshire, another inscription was discovered with excellently preserved Tartessian letters, and it then became clear that the Mount Hope inscription is also written in this style, though somewhat damaged by time, vandals and erosion. Under the outline carving of a hull appears a single line of Tartessian Punic, reading from right to left, to yield.

"VOYAGERS FROM TARSHISH THIS STONE PROCLAIMS"

"The script cannot of itself be accurately dated, but a likely estimate would perhaps be about 700 or 600 B.C. The voyagers were probably not explorers but rather merchants trading with the New England Celts who. by that date, would already be well-established fur trappers, and very likely also mining precious metals on those sites where ancient workings have been discovered." — (America B.C., p. 100)

The fate of some of the ships of Tarshish is postulated by Dr. Fell with the suggestion that they could still be found:

"What, then, became of the many ships of Tarshish that once frequented these same coasts from 2,000 to 3,000 years ago? Certainly some, probably many, must also lie on the bottom, for sea travel was more dangerous in ancient times, and the storm waves could surely wreak more havoc upon the timbered hulls of Phoenician galleys than on the steel plates of modern ships."

Fell agrees with Herm and Wiseman as to a large size and seaworthiness of the Tarshish ships:

"As to the relative sizes and strengths of ancient ships in comparison with those used by Columbus, medieval Europe of 1492 was in a stage of nautical skill that the ancients would have regarded as benighted. Columbus' whole expedition could mount only 88 men, carried on three vessels of which two were only 50 feet in length, about the size of a small Boston fish boat. Contrast that with the Pharaohs of the Ramesside dynasty, 1200 B.C., who could mount expeditions of 10,000 miners across the Indian Ocean to the gold-bearing lands of South Africa and Sumatra. Julius Caesar's triremes carried 200 men, yet he found his ships outmatched in size, height and seaworthiness by those of the maritime Celts." — (America B.C., p. 110)

The Celts who succeeded the Phoenicians in carrying on trade with the Americas lost their fleet to Julius Caesar in 55 B.C. and with the conquest by the Romans of Western Europe, the trading practices of the Celts with the Americas ceased and was in two centuries forgotten. Fell explains:

> "The entire Celtic fleet was destroyed or captured while the Romans still had 80 serviceable ships, with which Caesar later, in September of 55 B.C., carried the war across the Channel to Britannia.

> "There is no further mention of British or Gaulish naval vessels in Caesar's commentaries, nor does Tacitus in the century that followed give any space or consideration to native naval might. It seems that the battle against the Veneti was the end of Celtic sea power in classical times. Except for periodic truculence by British chiefs against Roman economic exploitation, for the most part the Celtic aristocracy willingly adopted Roman manners and luxury under the sweet persuasion of competent governors; and so the Celtic lands settled down to four centuries of relative prosperity and peace. By the time the Saxon pirates appeared off their eastern coasts, the Britons had forgotten their seamanship as well as most of their martial arts, and ruin soon followed, ushering in four more centuries of ignorance and misery." — (America B.C., p. 120)

Fell leaves no room for doubt about the fact of the merchants of Tarshish having established trading colonies in North America.

> "The men of Tarshish established colonies in eastern North America, the settlers probably drawn from the native Iberians

(that is, Celts and Basques) of the Guadalquivir valley in Andalusia.

"The first authenticated find of an engraved Phoenician tablet in an American archaeological context was that of a Tartessian inscription found in 1838. This tablet was excavated from a burial chamber found at the base of Mammoth Mound, in Moundsville, West Virginia. Although the Tartessian alphabet had not then been deciphered, the similarity of the inscription to Iberian writing was recognized, and in the contemporary reports of the dig, the mound and its contents were attributed to European visitors. Man-made burial mounds, or tumuli, are characteristic of many royal graves of the European Bronze Age.

"The notion that Europeans had visited and even settled in North America in ancient times continued as an acceptable hypothesis in the archaeological periodicals for the ensuing forty years. Then, sometime around 1870, the opinion became widespread that there had been no such callers before Columbus. The Moundsville tablet was forgotten, or dismissed as a later intrusion that had accidentally fallen into the mound, or been surreptitiously introduced by some irresponsible person." — (America B.C., p. 157)

The Phoenicians (of Tarshish), says Dr. Fell, penetrated deep within the American Continent, following the Mississippi up to what is now Davenport, Iowa.

"But it seems clear that Iberian and Punic-speakers were living in Iowa in the 9th century B.C., making use of a stone calendar regulator whose Egyptian hieroglyphs could apparently be read. The settlers had presumably sailed up the Mississippi River to colonize the Davenport area." — (America B.C., p. 268)

In conclusion, Fell offers the following summary:

"Various peoples from Europe and from northwest Africa sailed to America three thousand years ago and established colonies here. The primary evidence rests in the structures they built and in the inscriptions they wrote in letters that we now can identify as spelling phrases and sentences whose meaning we can grasp. — (America B.C., p. 288)

"The decipherments point to Iberia as the principal homeland of most of the wanderers who found their way to America in the millennium before Christ." — (America B.C., p. 289)

In the light of such conclusive scholarship, coming to light most significantly at this time when the nations indicated by Ezekiel as to be involved in a great Middle Eastern War, we can now say with definite assurance that The Merchants of Tarshish and "the young lions (colonies) thereof" must include the Western nations of Europe and the Americas, particularly the United States.

The fact that Israel's foreign minister Moshe Dayan has recently offered the United States military bases in Israel cannot be without great significance.

We hesitate to offer further conclusions. But if Ezekiel's prophecy is divinely given, and if we are to play fair with his

The bronze monument near Jerusalem which celebrates the fulfillment of the prophecy of the return of Israel, as recorded by Ezekiel in Chapters 36-37.

time indications, we have little choice but to infer that Ezekiel foresaw nations which in his time bore the titles, or were known then as, "Merchants of Tarshish" and "the young lions thereof." They are to be involved in confrontation with the Eastern European (Communist) bloc invaders of the Middle East. This is certainly reasonable to be possible in the not too distant future. Ezekiel's prophecy, which he claimed was given him from God, seems to indicate that this is exactly what will take place.

Because the outcome of this war will create great change in the balance of power and cause enormous international turmoil, it will reasonably give rise to a United Europe, formed by the diabolical statesmanship of the man known in the Scripture as the Antichrist.

The Antichrist and the Revival
of the Roman Empire

In 1922, Benito Mussolini, then an obscure editor of a socialist newspaper, led a revolution in Italy, which was ruled by a weak government and beset by economic stagnation following the war. His new government was called, "Fascism" after the "fasces," the symbol of the lictor of Ancient Roman cities. This new movement was also known as "National Socialism" and had as its goal the extension of Italian power and the resurrection and revival of the Roman Empire.

Mussolini's attempts at latter day Roman imperialism laid the ground work for the rise of Adolf Hitler and almost destroyed the world. World War II became inevitable because of the policies of these two types of fascism. But Mussolini lacked the character and Italy lacked the martial spirit to bring about his announced goals. He became known as "The Sawdust Caesar," the shadow of Hitler who was far more of a Caesar than his mentor.

For a time Mussolini's posturings gave rise to the suspicion that the Biblical prophecies concerning a revival of the Roman empire, as predicted in Daniel, would then come to pass. This notion faded with the destruction of the Third Reich and Fascism in Italy. Recently, however, it has again become a possibility in the establishment of the European Common Market.

The Coming Uniting of Europe

The emphasis upon the *economic* nature of the Common Market has revealed the need for European unity in marketing but in it are also the seeds of a political unity of Europe. Europe in the past has, through its stronger states, been a center of imperialism throughout the world. At one time the British Empire was the largest in history. Spain, France, Germany and Holland also possessed large empires. Now all are gone with the winds of anti-imperialism which have reduced all empires but that of the Soviet Union.

The disunity and provincialism of Europe has held this mighty continent of productive and talented people back from their potential destiny. Nationalism has been too important and language barriers and political rivalries have crippled them. Great wars between European countries have embroiled virtually the whole world at times. Today the spectre of communism has divided Europe within each country and serves to further prevent even an economic unity based upon the Common Market concept.

Given today's rapid transportation and communication, a United States of Europe is eminently feasible and if successful would make it the mightiest nation of states on earth. Several attempts to unite Europe by conquest and force of arms, notably by Adolph Hitler in this century, have failed. Not since the Holy Roman Empire and more effectively before that in the days of imperial Rome, has European hegemony been attempted with any success.

Today the need for unity is present but European nations continue to consider themselves as countries rather than states in a great European nation. Nothing presently in prospect seems to offer the *motivation* which would attract or force Europe into one nation.

But the Bible indicates this will change someday, perhaps even more swiftly than people can imagine.

World War III

The great unleashing of what will amount to World War III will come, as we have previously shown in prior chapters, according to the prophecy of Ezekiel 38-39, and will involve Western Europe in the conflict when Eastern Europe, led by Russians, moves to seize the oil fields of the Middle East.

As we have demonstrated, Europe is extremely vulnerable to the loss of Middle Eastern petroleum. It also faces Soviet expansionism. That Europe is incapable at present, and will be for the foreseeable future, of doing much more about Russia's invasion than to protest is very likely. But the given possibility of this seizure will doubtless do by fear what economics and common sense have been unable to do hitherto. Out of the Russian-led invasion, Europe, it seems likely, will finally unite and form a nation strong enough to insure economic security and political strength as the mightiest "nation" on earth.

This seems clear but it also seems highly unlikely, given present circumstances. Nevertheless, it is an obvious move in the light of what is coming.

The Shift in the Balance of Power

If Russia is defeated and drastically reduced as a world power, if, as the Bible indicates, part of eastern Europe is in ruins as the result of a nuclear attack, as Ezekiel's predictions hint, then there will be only two world powers left, the United States and a disciplined emerging Red China.

Europe will fear economic imperialism by the United States and, if famine should threaten the far east, will fear the military might of a hungry China with its hordes of soldiers whose Communist masters will not hesitate to sacrifice them by the millions if they are sufficiently motivated. Doubtless Communists within Europe itself will still be around to remind Europeans what it almost did.

This is the real prospect which will demonstrate to a frightened Europe that it *must* unite. Only if it is united, armed and working as one great nation can it become a world power to prevent the resurgence of communism or the attempt at global conquest by Red China.

The Leader Who Will Come

The person who will be the catalyst and leader of this new Europe is known in the Bible as the Antichrist. He will come from one of the nations which was part of the old Roman empire and will wage small wars of conquest and then by a satanical-inspired series of brilliant political maneuvers forge again the equivalent of a united Europe. From that base he will impose a peace upon the Middle East and move toward World Government, utilizing war, peace, deceit and his own tremendous personality to bring about world government.

Europe, therefore, being his base of operations, is destined to rise again to World prominence and power. The utter practicality of this scenario is now visible both from the point of view of Scripture prophecy and political realism. In a word, it is a workable scheme and the predictions of the Bible are now within the range of the clearly understandable in terms of the way nations tend to respond to challenge.

Europe is Moving Toward Unity

Europe is rife with godlessness and unbelief. Huge new suburbs are being built around its cities without churches. The religion of the past is losing its hold. Europe is fiercely devoted to pleasure, productivity and profit. It is ripe for a leader, given the very real threat which is now posed by Soviet imperialism. Far more dependent upon Middle Eastern oil than the United States of America, Europe is always within days of running out of petroleum, for it produces little on its own. Yet its whole system is based upon petroleum. Always this sword hangs over Europe, suspended by a very thin string.

Thus the realistic prospect of a Europe which is to be led by the Antichrist will reunite under one ruler as in the days of Ancient Rome.

The Biblical Teaching Concerning the Revival of the Roman Empire

There are four different and separate strands of Biblical knowledge and predictions concerning the revival of a "Romanized" Europe in the last days. We get the whole picture when these four strands come together:

1. Daniel's Vision of the Image — (Dan. 2:31-45)

2. Daniel's Vision of the Four Beasts — (Dan 7:1-27; 8:3-25)
   (Here the area from which the Antichrist will come is described as being part of both the ancient Greek and Roman empires which were in many places comingled.)

3. St. John's Vision of the Beast From The Sea — (Rev. 13:1-7)

4. St. John's Vision of the Doom of "Babylon" (i.e. Rome) — (Rev. 17:1-6, 9-18) (Rev. 18:1-2, 9,10,20,21,23,24)

SUMMARY

All of these visions from the most detailed portions of the pre-eminent prophetic portions of Daniel and the Revelation clearly indicate *Rome*. For Daniel, Rome was not yet a clear, present reality except in prophecy, since he lived at the time of early days of the Roman republic. Nevertheless, he was given the visions which predicted both ancient imperial Rome and the revival of the Roman Empire in the last days. This is abundantly clear and plain in his writings.

St. John, who lived during the Zenith of Rome's imperial power, could see more clearly the nature of Daniel's prophecy concerning Rome, upon which his own seem to have been projected, only more fully.

St. John used the term "Babylon" to stand for Rome because his book would come under the scrutiny of the Roman police authorities by whom the early Christians, even in John's time, had already suffered much. But he clearly indicated that "Babylon" stood for Rome in Rev. 17:9 where he identifies the "seven hills of Rome." Babylon itself is a "mystery" (Rev. 17:5), and again even more specifically as "that great City *which reigneth over the kings of the earth*" (Rev. 17:18) At the time John wrote, this could only mean Rome.

DR. WILLIAM STEUART McBIRNIE
Senior Minister
The United Community Church of Glendale,
California

Author, Biblical scholar, professor of church finance and church architecture, radio commentator, minister, humanitarian.

All of these terms describe Dr. William Steuart McBirnie, a man equally adept at delivering a moving sermon from the pulpit, lecturing in a graduate school classroom or personally supervising the distribution of medicine, food and other supplies to disaster victims in the far-flung corners of the free world.

In addition to his demanding duties as our Senior Minister he also serves as:

President of World Emergency Relief, a non-profit organization which provides aid to disaster victims on four continents.

Professor of church architecture at the California Graduate School of Theology, a school he helped found in 1968.

News analyst on the "Voice of Americanism," which is broadcast daily on a nationwide network of radio stations.

The author of more than 300 books and booklets on subjects ranging from Biblical subjects to national defense.

One of the founders of the INTERFAITH COMMITTEE, which is comprised of religious leaders and lay people throughout the world. Recent committee projects include opposition to commercialized blasphemy and to child molestation.

Born in Toronto, Canada, his father was a minister, his mother a concert cellist. He is an American citizen by choice, and is deeply devoted to his chosen country.

Dr. McBirnie is a graduate of the Southwestern Baptist Theological Seminary, and came to California in 1961 to become Senior Minister of the then newly-formed United Community Church. Under his guidance the membership has grown to more than 1,000 Christians from more than 30 denominations.

He has been knighted twice (Knights of Malta, Order of St. John) and was the second person to receive the Israeli Pilgrim's Medal, (Pope Paul was the first recipient). Dr. McBirnie is listed in "Who's Who in the Protestant Clergy" and "Who's Who in California." He was reported by the Gallup Poll as "one of the men Most Admired by the American People" for 1964.